DATE DUE

JAN 3 0 2005			

Crocheting

Written by
Gwen Blakley Kinsler and Jackie Young

Illustrated by
Esperança Melo

KIDS CAN PRESS

To Alan, Nicole and Bethany, my biggest fans — G.B.K.
To my parents, who have always encouraged my creativity — J.Y.

The projects in this book (with the exception of the Cozy lapghan)
were crocheted in Super 10 yarn distributed by S.R. Kertzer Limited.
For your nearest retail location visit www.kertzer.com or call (800) 263-2354.

Kids Can Press acknowledges the financial support of the Government of Canada,
through the BPIDP, for our publishing activity.

Published in Canada by	Published in the U.S. by
Kids Can Press Ltd.	Kids Can Press Ltd.
29 Birch Avenue	2250 Military Road
Toronto, ON M4V 1E2	Tonawanda, NY 14150

www.kidscanpress.com

Edited by Maggie MacDonald
Designed by Karen Powers
Photography by Frank Baldassarra
Printed in Hong Kong, China, by Wing King Tong Company Limited

The hardcover edition of this book is smyth sewn casebound.
The paperback edition of this book is limp sewn with a drawn-on cover.

CM 03 0 9 8 7 6 5 4 3 2 1
CM PA 03 0 9 8 7 6 5 4 3 2 1

National Library of Canada Cataloguing in Publication Data

Blakley Kinsler, Gwen, 1947–
Crocheting / written by Gwen Blakley Kinsler and Jackie Young ;
illustrated by Esperança Melo.

(Kids can do it)

ISBN 1-55337-176-3 (bound).   ISBN 1-55337-177-1 (pbk.)

1. Crocheting — Juvenile literature. I. Young Jackie, 1954–
II. Melo, Esperança III. Title. IV. Series.

TT820.B53 2003   j746.43'4   C2002-902088-3

Kids Can Press is a *Corus*™ Entertainment company

Contents

Introduction 4
Materials 4
Basic crochet techniques 6
Holding the yarn and hook 6
Slipknot 7
Chain stitch 8
Practicing stitches 9
Single crochet 9
Turning your work 10
Counting stitches 10
Adding new yarn 11
Fastening off 12
Finishing your work 12
Threading the yarn needle 13
Overcast stitch for sewing 14
Joining two pieces of crochet 15
Overhand knot 16
Adding the fringe 16
Daisy "chain" flowers 18
Fashion scarf 20
Bookmarks 22
Basic headband 24
Go anywhere purse 26
Sunglass caddy 30
Beaded belt 32
Beaded scrunchee 34
Cozy lapghan 36
Locker organizer 38

Introduction

Have you ever imagined that with just a crochet hook and some yarn you could create all the wonderful projects in this book, from doodling on your jeans with yarn to a cozy blanket for snuggling at a sleepover? This book uses the easiest crochet stitches, chain and single crochet, to make projects that are sure to please. Instructions help you get started and take you step-by-step through each project. A simple turn of the hook and twist of the yarn creates loops that are "hooked" together to create fun projects you can use every day or give as presents! And once you have learned the crochet stitches and practiced a bit, feel free to be as creative as you like. Surprise yourself by "doodling" with your yarn and hook!

MATERIALS

While you work on these projects, be sure to keep scissors, needles, crochet hooks and small items such as beads and buttons out of the reach of young children.

Yarn

Have you ever looked carefully at a length of yarn? It can feel smooth or rough, bumpy or furry. It comes in many different bright and cheerful colors, like a rainbow. Yarn can be made of many things, from sheep's wool to the fluffy white flower of the cotton plant. Yarn can also be made in a factory from acrylic fibers. Some yarns are heavy and some don't weigh much at all. Look at any leftover yarn at your house, or explore the many choices in a yarn or craft store. It is important to use the weight of yarn that the instructions suggest, such as worsted weight or sport weight. Choosing the color and type of yarn is up to you!

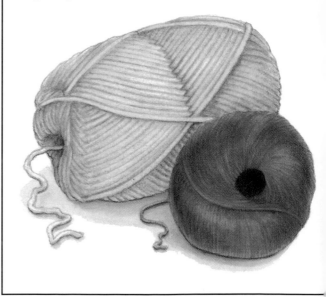

Crochet hooks

The word "crochet" is the French word for "hook." The crochet hook is a tool about the size of a pencil, with a hook on one end. Hooks come in all sizes and can be made of many things. Projects in this book use plastic or aluminum hooks. Each hook is marked with a number followed by "mm" for millimeters, a letter, or both, such as 5 mm (H), to indicate its size. Depending on the country of origin, the letter on the hook can vary.

It is important to match the size of hook with the weight of yarn you are using. Pattern instructions will help you decide which hook you should use. Since your yarn size determines the size of hook, choose your yarn first.

Yarn and sewing needles

You will need a yarn needle. It has a large eye, a blunt tip and is made of plastic or metal. For the headband, use a sharp needle with an eye that is big enough to be threaded easily and good quality polyester thread that matches your yarn. Be careful of the point on the needle!

Household supplies

Look around your house for scissors, a ruler or tape measure, safety pins, a small piece of elastic, hair elastics, cardboard, metal clips and fabric glue. You can also collect beads and buttons that will add sparkle to your projects.

Basic crochet techniques

As you are making your projects, refer to these pages whenever you need a reminder of how to do the stitches.

HOLDING THE YARN AND HOOK

Crochet is a two-handed craft. The left hand holds the yarn. The right hand moves the hook to create the stitches.

1. With the palm side of your left hand facing you, wrap the yarn, with the short end hanging free, around your little finger.

2. Now bring the yarn up to your index finger.

3. With the thumb and middle finger of your left hand, you can pinch the yarn close to the hook.

4. It is important to hold the yarn in your left hand in this way to create tension. Tension is the same as tightness and it helps you easily twist the yarn with the hook.

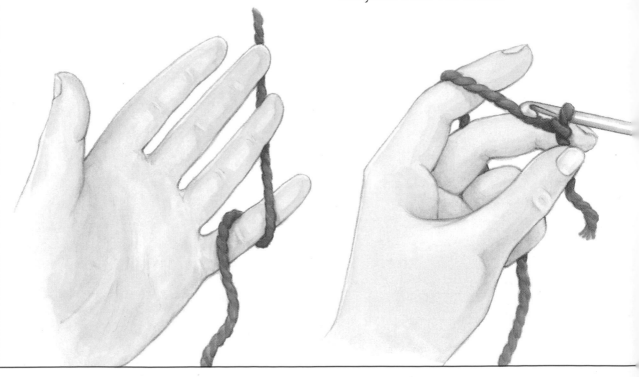

Your right hand is used to hold the hook in one of two positions:

Hold it as you would hold a pencil

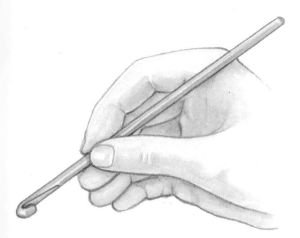

or hold it as you would clutch a tennis racket.

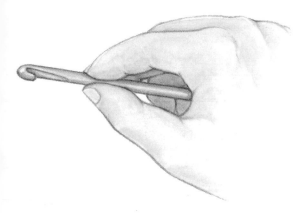

Try them both and use the position that feels most comfortable to you.

If you are left-handed, you can reverse the instructions by changing "right" to "left" and "left" to "right."

SLIPKNOT

Always begin your project with a slipknot.

1. Pull a 25 cm (10 in.) tail out from the ball of yarn, lay the yarn on a table and form two loops that look like the lower case letter "e."

2. Slide the first "e" on top of the second "e." This will look like a pretzel.

3. Pull the second "e" through the first "e." You now have a slipknot.

4. Insert the hook through this loop from front to back and pull gently until it tightens around the hook.

You are now ready to make chains.

CHAIN STITCH

Each chain stitch looks just like a link in a chain. Each one overlaps the next one. Have you seen the links on a dog's chain leash? They hook together, one inside the other, just like crochet chains.

1. Hold the slipknot with the thumb and middle finger of your left hand near the hook.

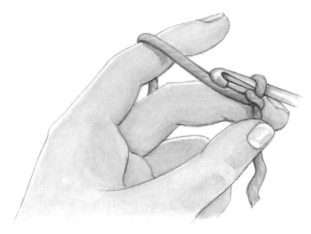

2. Holding the hook with your right hand, wrap the yarn around the hook from back to front.

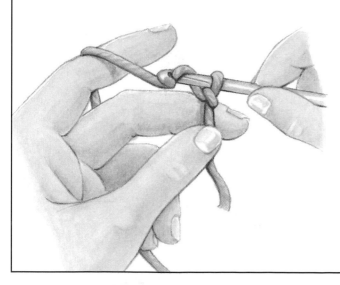

3. Turn the hook toward you and down to catch the yarn with the hook and pull it through the loop on the hook.

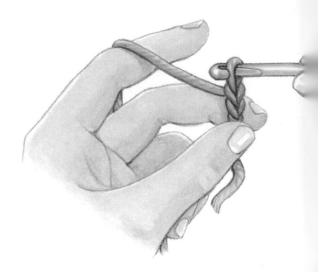

4. Move the thumb and middle finger of your left hand up to the knot of the stitch. You've made your first chain stitch!

5. Repeat steps 2–4 until the chain is the length you want it to be.

PRACTICING STITCHES

Do you know the saying, "Practice makes perfect"? The same is true with crocheting. To get comfortable with the chain stitch, have fun making a length of chain that can be stretched around the walls of your bedroom!

Now you are ready to try single crochet stitches. Remember when you learned to tie your shoes? It wasn't perfect the first time, but you practiced a lot and now you can do it without even thinking! Try out the stitches by making a sample piece before you start a project. When you are comfortable with the stitches, move on to the project.

SINGLE CROCHET

1. Insert the hook from front to back into the second chain stitch from the hook.

2. Wrap the yarn around the hook from back to front.

3. Pull the yarn through the loop on the hook. You now have two loops on the hook.

4. Holding your work tightly with the thumb and middle finger of your left hand, wrap the yarn over the hook from back to front and pull it through both of these loops.

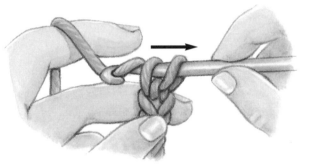

5. You now have one loop left on the hook, and the single crochet stitch is complete.

6. Repeat steps 1–5 to make a single crochet stitch in each chain stitch to the end of the chain.

TURNING YOUR WORK

1. After the first row of single crochet stitches is finished, start your next row by turning your work over as you would turn the pages of a book. Then make one chain stitch at the beginning of this new row.

2. Crocheting from right to left, your hook should go under the top two loops of each stitch. Be sure to make one single crochet stitch in each stitch of the previous row.

COUNTING STITCHES

Learning to count your stitches is easy once you get used to how they look. Chain stitches are easy to recognize as they are shaped like a **V**. That same **V** shape is part of the single crochet stitch. It can be seen at the top of each stitch.

• Look for the **V** and count each one in your beginning chain.

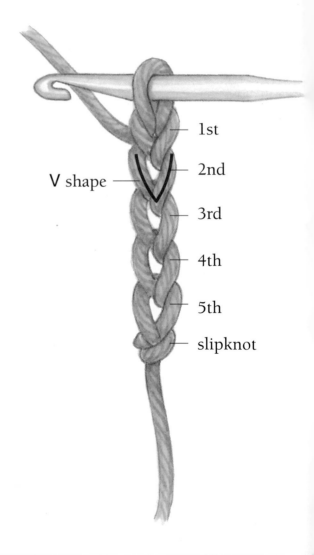

1st

V shape — 2nd

3rd

4th

5th

slipknot

- To count each single crochet stitch, look for the **V** at the top of each stitch.

- There will always be one loop on the hook when you crochet. Never count this loop.

— 1st
— 2nd
— 3rd
— 4th
— 5th

- Counting stitches is important in order to make sure that your project turns out the way you want it to.

ADDING NEW YARN

For some big projects, you may finish one ball or skein of yarn and need to add a new one. Join the new ball of yarn to your work whenever needed.

1. As you near the end of the ball, save enough yarn for one last stitch.

2. Start the last stitch with the old yarn.

3. Work the stitch as usual until there are two loops on your hook.

4. Finish the last steps of the stitch with the new yarn.

5. Leave a 10 cm (4 in.) tail of the new yarn hanging.

FASTENING OFF

When you complete a project, you will need to fasten off so that your work does not unravel, or come undone.

1. When you have completed your project, cut the yarn with the scissors leaving a 15 cm (6 in.) tail.

2. Bring the yarn over the hook from back to front. Pull the yarn all the way through the loop on the hook and then pull it tight to strengthen the knot.

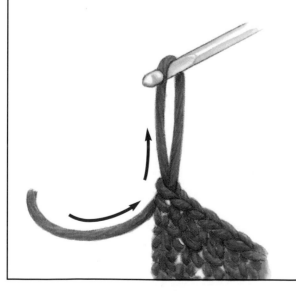

FINISHING YOUR WORK

1. Thread a yarn needle (page 13) onto the tail of yarn. Pull the end of the yarn under several stitches on the back of the project.

2. Now pull the yarn through several stitches in the opposite direction.

This is called "weaving," and it will prevent the project from unraveling.

THREADING THE YARN NEEDLE

1. Holding the yarn needle in your right hand, fold the yarn over the tip end of the needle.

2. With your left hand, pinch the yarn with your thumb and index finger very tightly against the needle.

3. Slide the needle out from the fold.

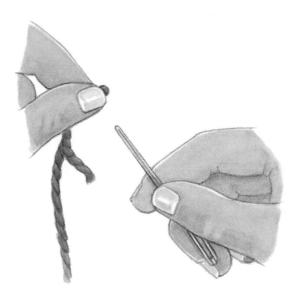

4. Continue holding the pinched yarn and slide it through the eye of the needle.

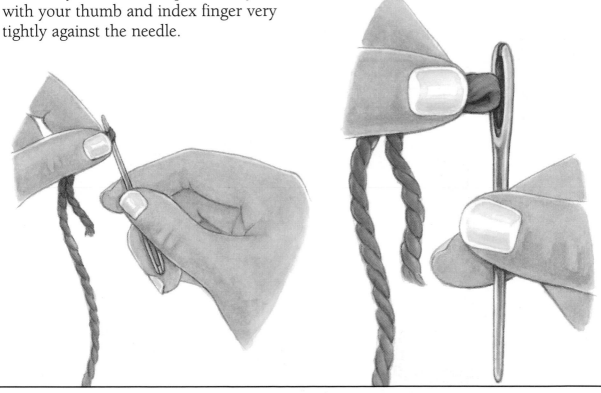

OVERCAST STITCH FOR SEWING

1. Knot the end of a 45 cm (18 in) length of yarn and thread it through your needle. Pull the needle toward you through two pieces of crochet fabric. Watch out for the point!

2. Bring the needle around the edge of the fabric layers.

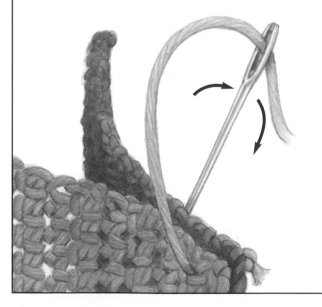

3. Poke the needle into the fabric layers again from the same side as the first stitch, but farther over. Keep stitching like this.

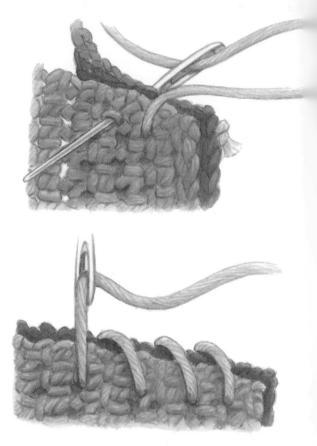

4. When you run out of yarn or reach the end, make two or three small stitches on or near the last stitch and cut the yarn.

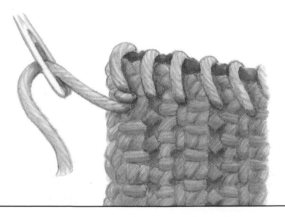

JOINING TWO PIECES OF CROCHET

1. Place the two finished pieces of crochet together, wrong (back) sides touching.

2. Pin the pieces so that they stay in place.

3. Attach the yarn to the hook with a slipknot. Pull the loop through both layers to the front and make a single crochet stitch.

4. Single crochet from right to left in each of the remaining stitches.

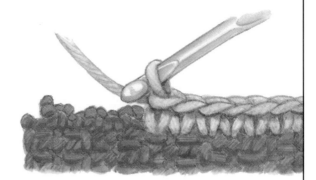

5. When both pieces are completely joined, fasten off (page 12).

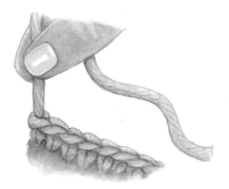

6. Remember: for smooth corners, always make three single crochet stitches in the same spot at each corner.

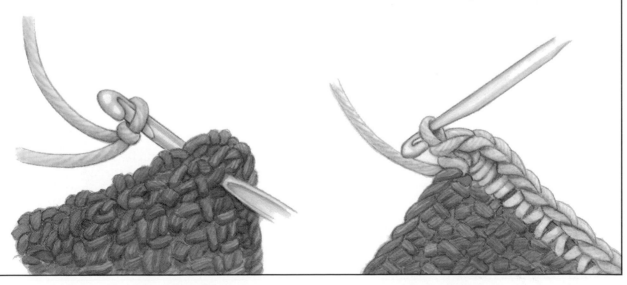

OVERHAND KNOT

1. Hold the yarn in your right hand.

2. Wrap the yarn in a circle around the index and middle fingers of your left hand.

3. Pull the tail end through the circle with your right hand.

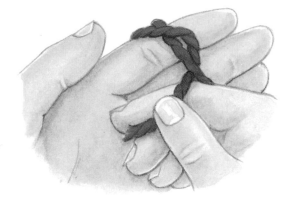

4. Tighten the knot.

ADDING THE FRINGE

1. Fold the required number of lengths of cut yarn in half.

2. Use the hook to pull the yarn through the stitches along the edge of the finished project.

3. Pull the yarn through the edge from right to wrong side.

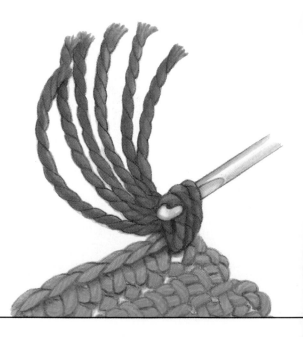

4. Draw the loose ends through the folded end.

6. Continue placing knots in this way evenly along the edge.

5. Pull on the loose ends to make a secure knot.

7. Trim the ends evenly with the scissors.

Daisy "chain" flowers

Make a whole bouquet of these colorful daisies and decorate a favorite shirt, pair of shoes or hat.

YOU WILL NEED

- a small amount worsted weight yarn
- 4.5 mm (G) crochet hook
- pony beads
- permanent fabric glue
- scissors, a ruler or tape measure, a yarn needle

1 Make a slipknot (page 7) and a 30 cm (12 in.) length of chain stitches (page 8).

2 Cut the yarn, leaving a 20 cm (8 in.) tail, and pull it through the last chain stitch on the hook to fasten off.

3 Wrap the chain around three fingers three times. Pinch the center to hold in place and remove from your fingers.

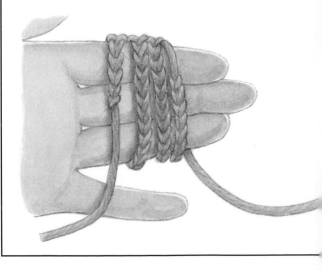

4 Wrap the 20 cm (8 in.) tail around the center of the chain bundle twice.

5 Thread the 20 cm (8 in.) tail through the eye of the yarn needle and pull or poke it up through the center of the chain bundle.

6 Thread a bead onto the yarn needle and go back down through the center to the back.

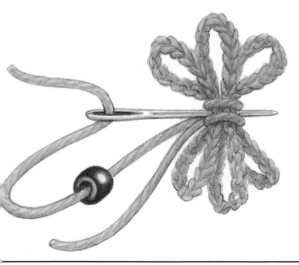

7 Make a knot and cut off the extra yarn.

8 Glue the flower onto your clothing, following the glue manufacturer's directions.

OTHER IDEAS

Make chains to form your initials, spirals, hearts and other squiggly shapes.

Fashion scarf

Crochet a bunch of these colorful scarves and make a fashion statement!

YOU WILL NEED

- 100 g (3½ oz.) worsted weight yarn
- 5.5 mm (I) crochet hook
- scissors, a ruler or tape measure, a yarn needle

1 Cut the fringe first. Find a book with a circumference of 30 cm (12 in.) and wrap the yarn around the book 20 times.

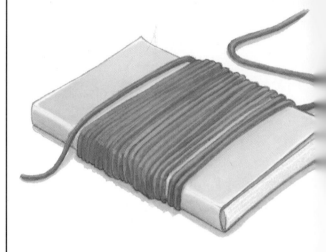

2 Cut through the wrapped yarn and set aside.

3 Make a slipknot (page 7) and 17 chain stitches (page 8). Single crochet (page 9) in the second chain from the hook and in each chain stitch to the end. You will have 16 single crochet stitches.

5 Using two lengths of yarn at a time, add five bunches of fringe (page 16) to each end of the scarf.

4 Making 16 single crochet stitches in each row, crochet until the scarf is 95 cm (38 in.) from the beginning chain. Remember to make one chain stitch at the beginning of each row. Fasten off (page 12).

Bookmarks

Celebrate a good book by using this special bookmark!

YOU WILL NEED

- 25 g (⅞ oz.) worsted weight yarn
- 4.5 mm (G) crochet hook
- small amounts of worsted weight and metallic yarn in contrasting colors (optional)
- pony beads and star beads (optional)
- a sewing needle and thread (optional)
- scissors, a ruler or tape measure, a yarn needle

1 Make a slipknot (page 7) and ten chain stitches (page 8). Single crochet (page 9) in the second chain stitch from the hook and in each chain stitch to the end. You will have nine single crochet stitches.

2 Making nine single crochet stitches in each row, work until the bookmark is 17.5 cm (7 in.) from the beginning chain stitch. Remember to make one chain stitch at the beginning of every row.

3 When the bookmark is long enough, don't cut the yarn. Work one more single crochet stitch in the stitch you just made.

4 Continue to single crochet down the long edge of the bookmark, making one single crochet stitch in every row until you get to the corner.

5 Work three single crochet stitches in the same spot. Single crochet along the short edge of the bookmark.

6 Make three single crochet stitches in the corner and then single crochet along the other long edge of the bookmark.

7 Work three single crochet stitches in the corner at the top of the bookmark. Single crochet along the last short edge, making two more single crochet stitches in the corner where you began. Fasten off (page 12).

DECORATIONS

Firecracker Bookmark

Crochet two curly tassels with the worsted weight yarn and one with the metallic yarn.

1. Make a slipknot (page 7) and 15 chain stitches (page 8). Beginning in the second chain stitch from the hook, make three single crochet stitches (page 9) in each chain stitch to the end. Fasten off (page 12), leaving a 12.5 cm (5 in.) tail.

2. Using the 12.5 cm (5 in.) tail, sew the curly tassels to the top of the bookmark with the yarn needle.

Flower Bookmark

Following steps 1–7 on pages 18–19, make a flower. Attach the flower to the bookmark with fabric glue.

Tassel Bookmark

Add three 25 cm (10 in.) lengths of fringe to the top edge of the bookmark (page 16). Add beads to the fringe and secure with an overhand knot (page 16).

Basic headband

This headband is all ready for your own special decorations!

YOU WILL NEED

- 50 g (1¾ oz.) worsted weight yarn in one color (A)
- small amount of worsted weight yarn in a contrasting color (B) for edging
- 4.5 mm (G) crochet hook
- a sewing needle and thread
- 4 cm (1.5 in.) length of elastic 5 cm (2 in.) wide
- scissors, a ruler or tape measure, a yarn needle

1 Measure your head and subtract 7.5 cm (3 in.) to determine how long to crochet the headband. Write the answer on a piece of paper.

2 Using color A, make a slipknot (page 7) and ten chain stitches (page 8). Single crochet (page 9) in the second chain from the hook and in each chain stitch to the end. You will have nine single crochet stitches.

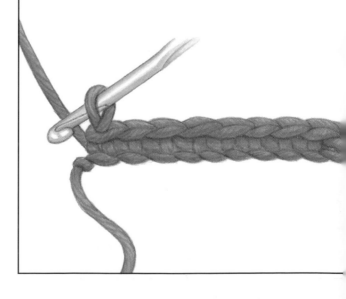

3 Make nine single crochet stitches in each row. Crochet until the headband is the measurement you took in step 1. Remember to make one chain stitch at the beginning of each row. Fasten off (page 12).

5 With the sewing needle and thread, sew the elastic to both ends of the headband.

4 Beginning in the last stitch you made, attach color B and single crochet all around the edge of the headband (steps 4–7, page 23). Fasten off.

OTHER IDEAS

Sew fun buttons onto your headband for a different look.

Go anywhere purse

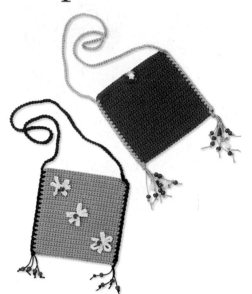

Here's a purse that's just the right size for carrying important stuff.

YOU WILL NEED

- 100 g (3 ½ oz.) worsted weight yarn in one color (A)
- 25 g (⅞ oz.) worsted weight yarn in a different color (B)
- 4.5 mm (G) crochet hook
- large safety pins
- a button
- pony beads and 1 cm (½ in.) star beads
- scissors, a ruler or tape measure, a yarn needle

1 Using color A, make a slipknot (page 7) and 27 chain stitches (page 8). Single crochet (page 9) in the second chain from the hook and in each chain stitch to the end. You will have 26 single crochet stitches in this row.

2 Making 26 single crochet stitches in each row, work until your purse is 30 cm (12 in.) from the beginning chain. Remember to make one chain stitch at the beginning of each row.

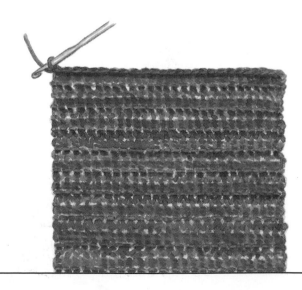

3 On the next row single crochet 13 stitches, crochet 10 chain stitches for the button loop and then single crochet the last 13 stitches in the row.

4 Cut the yarn, leaving a 12.5 cm (5 in.) tail, and pull it through the last loop on the hook to fasten off (page 12).

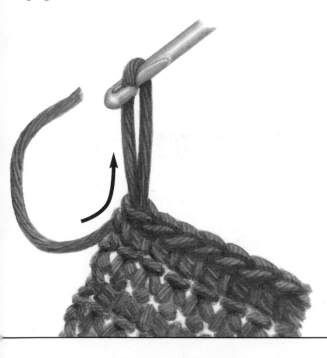

5 Fold the purse in half. Pin together with safety pins to hold in place.

6 Beginning at the lower right corner with color B, single crochet the front and back of purse together all the way to the top of the right edge of the purse (page 15).

Instructions continue on the next page ☞

7 Continue with the same yarn that is attached to the purse, making a 75 cm (30 in.) length of chain stitches.

8 Attach the chain that you just made to the upper left edge of the purse and continue to single crochet the front and back together down the left edge of the purse to the bottom left corner.

9 Cut the yarn, leaving a 12.5 cm (5 in.) tail, and pull it through the last loop on the hook to fasten off.

10 Cut six 25 cm (10 in.) lengths of yarn. Using three strands of yarn at a time add a fringe (page 16) to the bottom two corners of the purse.

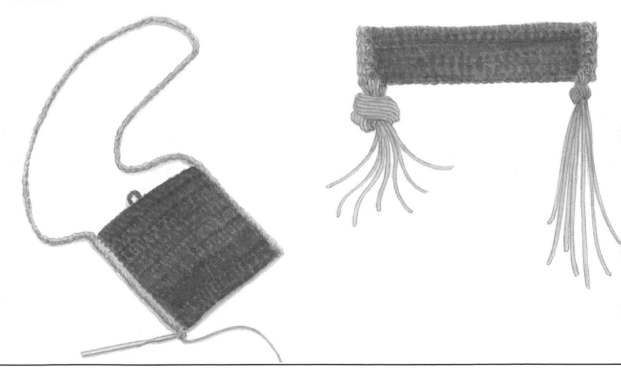

11 Thread pony beads and star beads onto the fringe and tie in place with an overhand knot (page 16). Sew a button to the front of the purse near the loop.

OTHER IDEAS

Make some extra daisy "chain" flowers (page 18) and glue them onto the purse for a different look.

Sunglass caddy

*A great place to stash your shades
when they're not in use.*

YOU WILL NEED

- 2 different-colored balls of
  worsted weight yarn,
  50 g (1¾ oz.) each color (A,B)
- 4.5 mm (G) crochet hook
- large safety pins
- scissors, a ruler or tape measure,
  a yarn needle

1   Using color A, make a slipknot
    (page 7) and 16 chain stitches
(page 8). Single crochet (page 9) in
the second chain from the hook and
in each chain stitch to the end. You
will have 15 single crochet stitches in
this row.

2   Work three more single crochet
    rows in color A, making sure you
have 15 single crochet stitches in each
row. Remember to make one chain
stitch at the beginning of each row.
Fasten off color A (page 12).

3   Work four single crochet rows in
    color B (Adding new yarn, page
11). Fasten off.

4 Using color A, work four single crochet rows. Fasten off.

5 Repeat steps 3 and 4 until you have a total of 20 stripes.

6 Fold the sunglass caddy in half and pin together with safety pins.

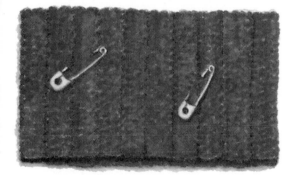

7 Using color A, make a 75 cm (30 in.) length of chain stitches. Do not fasten off.

8 With the chain hanging from the hook, crochet the front and back of the caddy together (page 15), beginning at the upper left corner. Continue down one side, around the bottom and up the other side. Leave the top edge open. Fasten off.

9 With the yarn needle, sew the beginning of the chain stitches to the upper right corner of the sunglass caddy and fasten off.

Beaded belt

Just the thing to complete an outfit.

YOU WILL NEED

- 3 different-colored balls of worsted weight yarn, 50 g (1¾ oz.) each color (A, B, C)
- 4.5 mm (G) crochet hook
- 60 pony beads
- scissors, a ruler or tape measure, a yarn needle

1 Using color A, make a slipknot (page 7) and 200 chain stitches (page 8). The chain should measure approximately 125 cm (50 in.) long. Fasten off (page 12).

2 Using color B, make 50 chain stitches. Do not fasten off, but continue by making a single crochet stitch (page 9) in the fifty-first chain stitch on the chain you made in step 1. Single crochet in 99 more chain stitches.

3 Finish the row by making 50 more chain stitches. Fasten off.

4 Repeat steps 2 and 3 with color C twice. There will be two rows of color C when you are done.

5 Repeat steps 2 and 3 with color B.

6 Repeat steps 2 and 3 with color A.

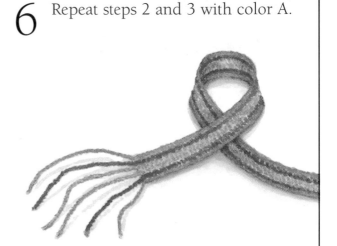

7 You now have a belt with a fringe made from the chain stitches on each end. Thread five pony beads onto each end of the fringe on both ends of the belt and secure with an overhand knot (page 16).

Beaded scrunchee

Now you're ready to try adding beads to this fun scrunchee.

1 Thread 24 pony beads onto the yarn. Push them up the yarn so they are out of the way for steps 2–4.

2 Put a slipknot (page 7) on the crochet hook.

3 Holding the elastic in your left hand, insert the hook in the center of the elastic, bring the yarn over the hook and pull it back through the elastic. You will now have two loops on the hook.

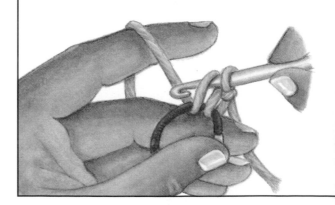

4 Bring the yarn over the hook again and pull it through both loops on the hook.

5 Repeat steps 3 and 4 until you have 25 single crochet stitches (page 9) evenly spaced over the elastic.

6 Make one single crochet in the first single crochet stitch you made.

7 Make two chain stitches, then slide a bead up to the crochet hook and make one chain stitch over the bead. Make two more chain stitches.

8 Make one single crochet stitch in the next stitch.

9 Repeat steps 7 and 8 until all the single crochet stitches have been used up and you have gone all the way around the elastic. Fasten off (page 12).

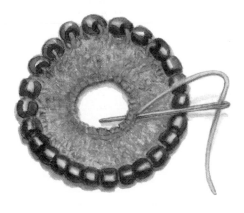

Cozy lapghan

Take this along on your next sleepover and you will be toasty warm while you watch movies and eat popcorn!

1 Using color A, make a slipknot (page 7) and 81 chain stitches (page 8). Single crochet (page 9) in the second chain from the hook and all remaining chain stitches. You will have 80 single crochet stitches.

2 Making 80 single crochet stitches in each row, work until the lapghan measures 120 cm (48 in.) from the beginning chain. Remember to make one chain stitch at the beginning of each row. Fasten off (page 12).

3 To make the fringe (page 16), find a book with a 30 cm (12 in.) circumference. Wrap color B around the book 66 times.

5 Repeat steps 3 and 4 with color C.

6 Using three lengths of yarn at a time, add 22 bunches of fringe to each short edge of the lapghan, alternating colors B and C.

4 Cut through the wrapped yarn and set aside.

Locker organizer

Get organized at school! Use the clips to attach important notes and pictures to your organizer.

YOU WILL NEED

- 100 g (3½ oz.) worsted weight yarn in one color (A)
- 2 different-colored balls of worsted weight yarn, 50 g (1¾ oz.) each color (B, C)
- 4.5 mm (G) crochet hook
- safety pins • 4 metal clips
- sturdy cardboard the size of your finished organizer
- scissors, a ruler or tape measure, a yarn needle

1 To make the front of the organizer, make a slipknot (page 7) and 36 chain stitches (page 8) using color A. Single crochet (page 9) in the second chain from the hook and all remaining chain stitches. You will have 35 single crochet stitches.

2 Making 35 single crochet stitches in each row, work until the front of the organizer is 25 cm (10 in.) from the beginning chain. Remember to make one chain stitch at the beginning of each row. Fasten off (page 12).

3 Repeat steps 1 and 2 to make the back of the organizer. Set the front and the back aside.

4 To make the pocket, make 17 chain stitches using color B. Single crochet in the second chain from the hook and the remaining chain stitches. You will have 16 single crochet stitches.

5 Making 16 single crochet stitches in each row, work until the pocket is 10 cm (4 in.) from the beginning chain. Fasten off.

6 Repeat steps 4 and 5 one more time with color B and two more times with color C. You will have four pockets in two different colors.

7 Lay the front of the organizer on a table. Pin one pocket in color B and one pocket in color C along the bottom edge of the organizer.

8 Using yarn to match the pockets, sew them both to the organizer, leaving the top edge open (page 14).

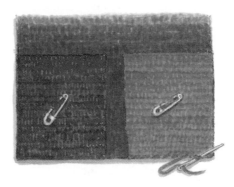

9 Leaving a 2.5 cm (1 in.) space above the first set of pockets, pin the remaining two pockets onto the organizer.

10 Sew the pockets to the organizer as in step 8. Remove the pins.

Instructions continue on the next page ☞

11 Lay the back of the organizer on a table. Place the front of the organizer on top of the back so you can see the pockets. Pin the front and the back together.

12 Using color A, single crochet the front and the back of the organizer together, beginning in the upper left corner (page 15). Leave the top edge open. Fasten off.

13 To make the strap, make 71 chain stitches using color A. Single crochet in the second chain stitch from the hook and all remaining chain stitches. You will have 70 single crochet stitches.

14 Making 70 single crochet stitches in each row, work until the strap is 2.5 cm (1 in.) from the beginning chain. Fasten off.

15 Pin the ends of the strap to the top of the organizer at each corner. Using color A, sew the strap to the organizer.

16 Put cardboard inside the organizer to make it sturdy. Put metal clips on the pockets.